MW00914860

YOUR COMPLETE LEO 2025 PERSONAL HOROSCOPE

Monthly Astrological Prediction Forecast Readings of Every Zodiac Astrology Sun Star Signs- Love, Romance, Money, Finances, Career, Health, Travel, Spirituality.

Iris Quinn

Alpha Zuriel Publishing

Your Complete Leo 2025 Personal Horoscope/ Iris Quinn. -- 1st ed.

"Astrology is a language. If you understand this language, the sky speaks to you."
— IRIS QUINN

CONTENTS

CHAPTER ONE

LEO PROFILE

General Characteristics

- **Element:** Fire
- **Quality:** Fixed
- **Ruler:** Sun
- **Symbol:** The Lion
- **Dates:** July 23 - August 22

Personality Traits

- **Charismatic:** Naturally attracts attention and admiration.
- **Confident:** Possesses strong self-assurance.
- **Ambitious:** Driven to achieve and excel.
- **Generous:** Warm-hearted and giving.
- **Loyal:** Devoted and faithful to loved ones.
- **Creative:** Imaginative and artistic.
- **Dramatic:** Enjoys being the center of attention.
- **Determined:** Perseveres in the face of challenges.

- **Optimistic:** Maintains a positive outlook on life.
- **Dominant:** Likes to take charge and lead.

Strengths

- **Leadership:** Natural-born leaders who inspire others.
- **Confidence:** Believes in their abilities and worth.
- **Generosity:** Willing to help and support others.
- **Creativity:** Comes up with innovative and artistic ideas.
- **Loyalty:** Stands by friends and family through thick and thin.
- **Charisma:** Attracts people with their magnetic personality.

Weaknesses

- **Stubbornness:** Resistant to change and compromise.
- **Arrogance:** Can be overly proud and self-centered.
- **Dominance:** May try to control situations and people.
- **Impatience:** Desires quick results and can be easily frustrated.
- **Dramatic:** Can be overly emotional or theatrical.

Planets and Their Influences

- **Career Planet:** Saturn – Provides discipline and structure in professional life.
- **Love Planet:** Venus – Governs affection, beauty, and romantic relationships.
- **Money Planet:** Venus – Influences financial matters and luxury.
- **Planet of Fun, Entertainment, Creativity, and Speculations:** Jupiter – Encourages joy and creativity.
- **Planet of Health and Work:** Mercury – Influences routine, health, and communication.
- **Planet of Home and Family Life:** Moon – Governs emotions and domestic affairs.
- **Planet of Spirituality:** Neptune – Represents dreams, intuition, and spiritual pursuits.
- **Planet of Travel, Education, Religion, and Philosophy:** Jupiter – Governs growth, learning, and philosophical outlooks.

Compatibility

- **Signs of Greatest Overall Compatibility:** Aries, Sagittarius
- **Signs of Greatest Overall Incompatibility:** Taurus, Scorpio
- **Sign Most Supportive for Career Advancement:** Capricorn
- **Sign Most Supportive for Emotional Well-being:** Libra
- **Sign Most Supportive Financially:** Virgo
- **Sign Best for Marriage and/or Partnerships:** Aquarius

- **Sign Most Supportive for Creative Projects:** Gemini
- **Best Sign to Have Fun With:** Aries
- **Signs Most Supportive in Spiritual Matters:** Pisces
- **Best Day of the Week:** Sunday

Additional Details

- **Colors:** Gold, Orange
- **Gem:** Ruby
- **Scent:** Citrus, Sandalwood
- **Birthstone:** Peridot
- **Quality:** Fixed (resolute and determined)

PERSONALITY OF LEO

Leo, born between July 23 and August 22, is a fire sign ruled by the Sun. This connection to the Sun infuses Leo with warmth, radiance, and a natural charisma that makes them stand out in any crowd. Leos are known for their vibrant personality, which combines confidence, ambition, and a generous spirit. They have an innate ability to attract attention and admiration, often becoming the center of any social gathering.

Leos are inherently confident and self-assured. They believe in their abilities and are not afraid to pursue their goals with determination and passion. This confidence often makes them natural leaders, capable of inspiring and motivating those around them. They thrive in positions of authority where they can showcase their leadership skills and take charge of situations. Their ambition drives them to aim high and achieve great things, as they are not content with mediocrity.

Generosity is a hallmark of the Leo personality. They have a big heart and are always willing to help those in need. Whether it's offering support to a friend or contributing to a cause they believe in, Leos are known for their warm-hearted and giving nature. They take great joy in making others happy and are often seen as the protector of their loved ones, always ready to lend a helping hand or provide comfort.

Creativity is another defining trait of Leo. They have a vivid imagination and a strong sense of artistry. This creative energy can manifest in various forms, from artistic pursuits like painting, music, or theater, to innovative problem-solving in their professional lives. Leos love to express themselves and often do so with flair and originality, adding a touch of drama and excitement to everything they do.

Loyalty is deeply ingrained in the Leo character. They are fiercely loyal to their friends and family, standing by them through thick and thin. Once they commit to someone, whether it's in friendship or love, they are devoted and steadfast. This loyalty makes them reliable partners and friends, who can be counted on for their unwavering support.

Despite their many positive traits, Leos can also have a few challenging aspects to their personality. Their confidence can sometimes border on arrogance, making them appear self-centered or overly proud.

They enjoy being in the spotlight and can become frustrated if they feel ignored or undervalued. This need for attention and admiration can lead to a dominant and controlling demeanor, where they try to assert their will over others.

Leos can also be quite stubborn. Once they have set their mind on something, it's hard to change their course. This resoluteness can be both a strength and a weakness, as it helps them achieve their goals but can also make them inflexible and resistant to change. Additionally, their dramatic nature can sometimes result in emotional outbursts or exaggerated reactions, especially when they feel challenged or threatened.

In relationships, Leos are passionate and enthusiastic partners. They bring warmth, excitement, and a sense of adventure to their romantic connections. They seek partners who can match their energy and who appreciate their grand gestures of love and affection. Leos need to feel adored and respected, and they thrive in relationships where they are given the admiration they crave. However, they also need to learn to share the spotlight and appreciate the strengths and contributions of their partner.

Leos have a positive outlook on life. They are optimistic and upbeat, always looking for the silver lining in any situation. This positive energy is contagious and can uplift those around them, making them enjoyable and inspiring companions. Their enthusiasm for life is matched by their determination to overcome challenges and bounce back from setbacks with resilience and strength.

Overall, Leos are dynamic, confident, and generous individuals who bring warmth and vitality to any situation. Their leadership, creativity, and loyalty make them natural-born leaders and cherished friends. While they may need to temper their stubbornness and desire for attention, their positive qualities shine brightly, making them a powerful and influential presence in the lives of those they touch.

WEAKNESSES OF LEO

Leo, while possessing many admirable qualities, also has weaknesses that can sometimes pose challenges in their personal and professional lives. One of the most significant weaknesses of Leo is their tendency towards arrogance. Their natural confidence and charisma can sometimes tip over into a sense of superiority. They may come across as overly proud or self-important, which can alienate others and create tension in relationships. Leos need to be mindful of this tendency and strive to balance their self-assurance with humility and respect for others' contributions.

Another notable weakness of Leo is their desire for constant attention and admiration. They thrive on being in the spotlight and can become frustrated or even despondent if they feel ignored or underappreciated. This need for validation can make them dependent on external approval, which can be exhausting for those around them. Leos need to learn to find internal validation and appreciate their own worth without always seeking affirmation from others.

Leos are also known for their stubbornness. Once they set their mind on something, it is difficult to change their opinion or course of action. This resoluteness can be a double-edged sword. While it helps them achieve their goals, it can also make them inflexible and resistant to new ideas or perspectives. They may struggle to adapt to changing circumstances or to compromise in situations that require flexibility. Learning to be more open-minded and willing to consider alternative viewpoints can help Leos navigate this challenge.

Additionally, Leos can be quite dramatic in their emotional expressions. They feel things intensely and are not afraid to show it. This dramatic flair can sometimes lead to exaggerated reactions or emotional outbursts, particularly when they feel their pride is wounded or their authority is challenged. Their dramatic nature can be overwhelming for those around them, making it important for Leos to practice emotional regulation and find healthy outlets for their intense feelings.

In relationships, Leos' strong desire to lead and dominate can sometimes create imbalances. They may unintentionally overshadow their partners, seeking to assert their will and take control of situations. This can lead to conflicts and feelings of resentment if their partner feels undervalued or sidelined. Leos need to be conscious of their dominant tendencies and make an effort to ensure their relationships are based on mutual respect and equality.

Another challenge for Leo is their impatience. They desire quick results and can become easily frustrated when things do not progress as swiftly as they would like. This impatience can lead to rash decisions and a lack of thorough planning, which can undermine their efforts in the long run. Leos benefit from learning to cultivate patience and an appreciation for the process, understanding that success often requires time and perseverance.

Furthermore, Leos can be highly self-critical. Despite their outward confidence, they can be deeply affected by failures and criticisms, sometimes taking these setbacks very personally. This sensitivity can lead to a fear of failure, making them hesitant to take risks or try new things. Building resilience and developing a more balanced view of success and failure can help Leos manage this vulnerability.

While Leos are naturally generous and giving, their generosity can sometimes come with strings attached. They may expect recognition and gratitude in return for their kindness, and if this is not forthcoming, they can feel slighted or unappreciated. Learning to give without expectations and finding satisfaction in the act of giving itself can help mitigate this tendency.

In summary, the weaknesses of Leo, such as arrogance, need for attention, stubbornness, dramatic tendencies, impatience, and sensitivity to criticism, can present challenges in their interactions with others and in their personal growth. By becoming aware of these traits and working to balance them with humility, openness, and emotional regulation, Leos can harness their strengths more effectively and build more harmonious relationships. Their journey towards self-awareness and growth involves embracing both their powerful qualities and their vulnerabilities, creating a more balanced and fulfilling life.

RELATIONSHIP COMPATIBILITY WITH LEO

Based only on their Sun signs, this is how Leo interacts with others. These are the compatibility interpretations for all 12 potential Leo combinations. This is a limited and insufficient method of determining compatibility.

However, Sun-sign compatibility remains the foundation for overall harmony in a relationship.

The general rule is that yin and yang do not get along. Yin complements yin, and yang complements yang. While yin and yang partnerships can be successful, they require more effort. Earth and water zodiac signs are both Yin. Yang is represented by the fire and air zodiac signs.

Leo with Yang Signs (Fire and Air)

Leo and Aries (Yang with Yang):

Leo and Aries are a powerful and dynamic pairing. Both signs are energetic, passionate, and love adventure, making their relationship vibrant and full of excitement. Leo's confidence and charisma complement Aries' boldness and enthusiasm. They inspire and motivate each other, creating a dynamic partnership that thrives on mutual admiration and respect. However, their strong personalities can lead to power struggles if neither is willing to compromise. To maintain harmony, they need to practice patience, learn to share the spotlight, and appreciate each other's strengths.

Leo and Sagittarius (Yang with Yang):

Leo and Sagittarius form a naturally compatible and adventurous duo. Both signs are optimistic, energetic, and love exploring new experiences. Sagittarius' philosophical outlook and sense of humor blend well with Leo's warmth and enthusiasm. They enjoy a relationship filled with fun, excitement, and mutual inspiration. The only potential downside is their tendency to be blunt, which can sometimes hurt each other's feelings. However, their mutual understanding and love for adventure generally help them overcome any minor conflicts, making this a vibrant and fulfilling partnership.

Leo and Gemini (Yang with Yang):

The relationship between Leo and Gemini is lively and intellectually stimulating. Gemini's curiosity and adaptability complement Leo's charisma and leadership. They enjoy engaging in deep conversations and social activities, keeping their relationship fresh and dynamic. Leo can sometimes be frustrated by Gemini's indecisiveness, while Gemini may find Leo too domineering. To make this pairing work, they need to appreciate each other's strengths—Gemini's communicative skills and Leo's decisiveness—and find a balance between flexibility and action. Open communication and mutual respect are key to maintaining harmony.

Leo and Leo (Yang with Yang):

When two Leos come together, the relationship is intense, passionate, and full of energy. Both partners share a love for excitement, creativity, and leadership. They understand each other's need for admiration and thrive on mutual respect and affection. However, their similar traits can lead to frequent clashes, as both can be stubborn and desire to be in control. To make this relationship work, they need to learn patience, compromise, and how to balance their competitive natures. Communication and mutual respect are key to maintaining harmony in this powerful pairing.

Leo and Libra (Yang with Yang):

Leo and Libra create a dynamic and balanced relationship. Libra's charm, diplomacy, and love for harmony complement Leo's assertiveness and confidence. Libra can help Leo slow down and consider different perspectives, while Leo adds excitement and initiative to Libra's life. Their relationship thrives on the attraction of opposites, but Leo's directness can sometimes clash with Libra's desire for peace, leading to occasional conflicts. Communication and understanding are essential for maintaining harmony. By learning to appreciate their differences, they can create a harmonious and fulfilling partnership.

Leo and Aquarius (Yang with Yang):

Leo and Aquarius share a love for independence, innovation, and adventure. Aquarius' visionary ideas and unconventional approach to life attract Leo, who admires their originality and intellect. Leo's courage and action-oriented nature inspire Aquarius, creating a relationship that is both exciting and intellectually stimulating. They enjoy exploring new ideas and experiences together, keeping their relationship fresh and dynamic. However, both signs value their freedom, which can sometimes lead to a lack of emotional closeness. They need to work on maintaining a strong emotional connection while respecting each other's need for independence.

Leo with Yin Signs (Earth and Water)

Leo and Taurus (Yang with Yin):

Leo and Taurus have contrasting energies that can make their relationship challenging but rewarding. Leo is spontaneous and adventurous, while Taurus is steady, practical, and values security. Leo can bring excitement and a sense of adventure to Taurus's life, encouraging them to step out of their comfort zone. Conversely, Taurus can offer Leo stability and patience, helping them to appreciate the finer details of life. For this relationship to work, both partners need to be willing to understand and appreciate their differences. Leo should be more considerate of Taurus's need for stability and routine, while Taurus should be open to change and new experiences.

Communication and mutual respect are crucial for creating a balanced and enriching partnership.

Leo and Virgo (Yang with Yin):

Leo and Virgo have very different approaches to life, which can create friction but also offer opportunities for growth. Leo is impulsive, action-oriented, and loves taking risks, while Virgo is analytical, methodical, and prefers careful planning. Leo might find Virgo's attention to detail and cautious nature frustrating, while Virgo might see Leo as reckless and inconsiderate. However, if they can learn from each other, this relationship can be complementary. Leo can benefit from Virgo's organizational skills and practical approach, while Virgo can be inspired by Leo's boldness and willingness to take risks. Patience, understanding, and a willingness to compromise are essential for making this pairing work.

Leo and Capricorn (Yang with Yin):

Leo and Capricorn have a challenging yet potentially rewarding relationship. Leo is spontaneous and seeks immediate results, while Capricorn is disciplined, focused on long-term goals, and prefers a structured approach. These differing outlooks can lead to misunderstandings and conflicts. However, if they can appreciate each other's strengths, they can form a powerful team. Leo can bring energy and enthusiasm to Capricorn's plans, injecting a sense of urgency and excitement. Conversely, Capricorn can provide the structure and persistence that Leo needs to achieve their goals. This relationship requires patience, compromise, and a willingness to understand each other's perspectives. When they work together, they can achieve great things.

Leo and Cancer (Yang with Yin):

Leo and Cancer have contrasting needs and approaches that can make their relationship challenging but potentially very rewarding. Leo is independent, assertive, and often focuses on their own goals, while Cancer is sensitive, nurturing, and seeks emotional connection and security. Leo can sometimes be too direct and forceful for Cancer's delicate nature, leading to hurt feelings. However, if they learn to appreciate each other's differences, they can form a complementary partnership. Leo can bring excitement and courage to Cancer's life, encouraging them to step out of their emotional comfort zone. In return, Cancer can provide emotional support and care, teaching Leo the value of empathy and nurturing. Mutual understanding and respect are essential to making this relationship work.

Leo and Scorpio (Yang with Yin):

Leo and Scorpio have a relationship filled with intensity and passion. Both signs are strong-willed, determined, and possess a deep emotional connection, which can create a powerful and transformative bond. Leo is drawn to Scorpio's mysterious and intense nature, while Scorpio appreciates Leo's courage and straightforwardness. However, their mutual desire for control and dominance can lead to power struggles and conflicts. To make this relationship work, they need to be mindful of their tempers, learn to compromise, and respect each other's strengths. When they work together, they can achieve great things and create a deeply fulfilling and passionate relationship.

Leo and Pisces (Yang with Yin):

Leo and Pisces have very different natures that can make their relationship challenging but potentially rewarding. Leo is bold, assertive, and action-oriented, while Pisces is gentle, introspective, and driven by their emotions. Leo can sometimes be too aggressive for Pisces' sensitive nature, leading to misunderstandings and hurt feelings. However, if they learn to appreciate each other's differences, they can form a complementary partnership. Leo can help Pisces be more confident and assertive, encouraging them to pursue their dreams actively. In return, Pisces can teach Leo about compassion, creativity, and the value of emotional connection. This relationship requires patience, understanding, and a willingness to learn from each other.

In conclusion, Leo's compatibility with other sun signs varies widely based on the yin and yang theory. Fire and air signs generally complement Leo's energetic and charismatic nature, leading to vibrant and exciting relationships. Earth and water signs, while presenting more challenges, can provide balance and stability, requiring more effort to navigate their differences. With mutual respect, understanding, and a willingness to learn from each other, Leo can form successful and fulfilling partnerships with any sign.

LOVE AND PASSION

Love and passion for Leo are intertwined with their vibrant and charismatic nature. Governed by the Sun, Leos are naturally warm-hearted, enthusiastic, and expressive in their romantic relationships. They approach love with a grand and generous spirit, often viewing their romantic life as a stage where they can shine and express their deepest emotions. Leo's love is not quiet or subdued; it is bold, dramatic, and filled with a fervent desire to create memorable experiences.

When Leo falls in love, they do so with their entire being. Their passion is evident in every gesture, word, and action. They are incredibly devoted and seek to make their partner feel like the most special person in the world. Leo's romantic gestures are often grand and extravagant, as they take great joy in spoiling their loved ones with gifts, surprises, and heartfelt declarations of love. They are not shy about showing their affection and expect their partner to reciprocate with the same level of enthusiasm and devotion.

Leo thrives on admiration and appreciation. They need to feel valued and respected in their relationships, and they seek partners who can celebrate their achievements and acknowledge their efforts. This need for validation stems from their deep-seated desire to be recognized and adored. In return, Leo is incredibly loyal and protective of their partner, often going to great lengths to ensure their happiness and well-being. They see their relationship as a partnership where both individuals uplift and support each other.

Passion for Leo is a multifaceted experience. It encompasses not only physical attraction but also emotional and intellectual connection. They seek a partner who can match their energy and enthusiasm, someone who is equally passionate about life and love. Leos are drawn to individuals who are confident, ambitious, and capable of engaging them in stimulating conversations. They appreciate a partner who can keep up with their dynamic lifestyle and who shares their zest for adventure and exploration.

In the realm of intimacy, Leo is a generous and attentive lover. They take pride in pleasing their partner and are highly responsive to their needs and desires. Their sensuality is expressed through touch, affection, and a deep desire to connect on a profound level. Leo's passion in the bedroom is characterized by a blend of tenderness and intensity, creating an experience that is both exhilarating and deeply satisfying. They are creative and adventurous, always looking for ways to keep the spark alive and make their intimate moments memorable.

However, Leo's intense passion can also be challenging at times. Their strong emotions and desire for control can lead to conflicts if not managed with care. They can be demanding and expect a high level of attention and devotion from their partner. If they feel neglected or undervalued, their fiery nature can manifest in dramatic displays of frustration or anger. It is important for their partner to understand this aspect of Leo's personality and to provide the reassurance and affirmation they crave.

Despite their dominant personality, Leos have a vulnerable side that they often keep hidden. They fear rejection and can be deeply hurt by criticism or indifference. Beneath their confident exterior lies a need for emotional security and a fear of being unloved. When they feel truly loved and appreciated, they become even more generous and devoted, creating a relationship that is rich in warmth, loyalty, and mutual respect.

Leo's approach to love is also influenced by their creative and artistic nature. They enjoy bringing a touch of romance and drama into their relationships, often planning elaborate dates, romantic getaways, and thoughtful surprises. They see love as an art form, something to be nurtured and celebrated with passion and creativity. This artistic flair adds a unique and enchanting quality to their relationships, making them feel like a beautiful and exciting journey.

In conclusion, love and passion for Leo are vibrant, intense, and deeply fulfilling. They bring a sense of warmth, generosity, and excitement to their relationships, seeking partners who can match their enthusiasm and devotion. Their need for admiration and appreciation drives them to be loyal and protective lovers, always striving to make their partner feel cherished and adored. While their intense passion can sometimes lead to challenges, their deep capacity for love and their creative approach to romance make them unforgettable partners who can create a deeply satisfying and dynamic relationship.

MARRIAGE

Marriage for Leo is a grand and passionate affair, filled with warmth, loyalty, and a desire for mutual admiration. Governed by the Sun, Leos bring a radiant and enthusiastic energy to their marital relationships. They view marriage as a partnership where both individuals shine together, creating a life that is vibrant and full of love. To keep a Leo happy in marriage, it is essential to understand their need for recognition, appreciation, and affection. Leos thrive on admiration and need to feel valued and respected by their partner. They appreciate grand gestures of love and heartfelt expressions of admiration, which make them feel cherished and special.

Leo men in marriage are typically confident, charismatic, and deeply devoted to their spouses. They take pride in their role as a husband and often see themselves as the protector and provider in the relationship. A Leo man is generous with his affection and enjoys spoiling his partner with gifts, surprises, and romantic gestures. He seeks a partner who can appreciate his efforts and reciprocate with love and loyalty. To keep a Leo man happy in marriage, it is crucial to acknowledge his achievements and express gratitude for his efforts. He values a partner who can support his ambitions and share in his successes, creating a harmonious and mutually supportive relationship. Encouraging his creative pursuits and participating in activities that he enjoys also helps to strengthen the bond and keep the relationship dynamic and exciting.

Leo women in marriage bring a similar level of enthusiasm, creativity, and devotion to their relationships. They are often the heart of the home, creating a warm and loving environment for their family. A Leo woman values emotional connection and seeks a partner who can match her passion and energy. She is loyal and protective of her loved ones and expects the same level of commitment from her partner. To keep a Leo woman happy in marriage, it is important to shower her with affection and appreciation. She thrives on compliments and needs to feel adored and respected. Supporting her in her personal and professional endeavors and celebrating her achievements helps to reinforce the emotional bond and create a fulfilling partnership.

The secret to making a marriage with Leo work lies in understanding and honoring their need for admiration and mutual respect. Leos are deeply sensitive to criticism and can be easily hurt by perceived slights or neglect. It is essential to communicate openly and honestly, expressing love and appreciation regularly. Leos also value loyalty and expect their partner to be as committed and devoted as they are. Trust and honesty are the cornerstones of a successful marriage with Leo, as they need to feel secure and confident in their partner's love and support.

Another key aspect of maintaining a happy marriage with Leo is to keep the relationship exciting and dynamic. Leos love adventure and enjoy trying new things, whether it is exploring new hobbies, traveling, or engaging in creative projects. Sharing these experiences with their partner helps to keep the relationship fresh and invigorating. Planning romantic getaways, celebrating milestones, and creating special moments together can help to strengthen the bond and keep the passion alive.

Leos also appreciate a sense of balance in the relationship. While they enjoy being the center of attention, they also value a partner who can stand confidently by their side and share in the responsibilities of life. Encouraging each other's growth and supporting each other's dreams helps to create a balanced and harmonious partnership. Leos are natural leaders and enjoy taking charge, but they also need a partner who can challenge them and provide a different perspective, helping them to grow and evolve.

In moments of conflict, it is important to approach Leo with sensitivity and understanding. They can be fiercely proud and may react strongly to criticism. Using constructive communication and focusing on positive reinforcement helps to resolve conflicts more effectively. Showing empathy and being willing to compromise can help to navigate challenges and maintain harmony in the relationship.

In summary, marriage with Leo is a vibrant and passionate journey that requires mutual admiration, respect, and a shared sense of adventure. By understanding and honoring their need for recognition and affection, providing unwavering loyalty and support, and keeping the relationship dynamic and exciting, one can create a deeply fulfilling and lasting partnership with Leo. Their warm-hearted and generous nature, combined with their enthusiasm and creativity, makes them dedicated and loving partners who bring a sense of joy and excitement to their marriages.

CHAPTER TWO

LEO 2025 HOROSCOPE

Overview Leo 2025

(July 23 - August 22)

The year 2025 promises to be a significant one for Leos, with various planetary transits and celestial events influencing different aspects of your life. Let's dive into the details and explore what the stars have in store for you.

The year begins with Mars entering Leo on April 18th, bringing a surge of energy, passion, and motivation. This is an excellent time to take initiative, start new projects, and assert yourself in your personal and professional life. With Mars in your sign until June 17th, you'll have the drive and confidence to pursue your goals and make your mark on the world.

In mid-June, Saturn briefly shifts into Aries, activating your 9th house of higher learning, philosophy, and spiritual growth. This transit may bring challenges or responsibilities related to your beliefs, education, or long-distance connections. It's essential to remain disciplined and committed to your personal growth during this time.

On July 22nd, the Sun, your ruling planet, enters your sign, marking the beginning of your birthday season. This is a time to celebrate your unique qualities, recharge your batteries, and set intentions for the year ahead. Embrace your creativity, leadership skills, and zest for life during this empowering period.

The Partial Solar Eclipse in Virgo on September 21st will occur in your 2nd house of finances and material resources. This eclipse may bring changes or new opportunities related to your income, possessions, or self-worth. It's a great time to reassess your values, set financial goals, and make practical plans for the future.

In late September, Mars enters Libra, your 3rd house of communication and learning. This transit can bring increased mental energy, curiosity, and a desire to connect with others. It's an excellent time to network, learn new skills, and express your ideas with confidence and clarity.

On October 22nd, the Sun enters Scorpio, highlighting your 4th house of home, family, and emotional foundation. This is a time to focus on your inner world, nurture your close relationships, and create a supportive and nurturing living space. Honor your emotional needs and prioritize self-care during this introspective period.

In mid-November, Venus enters Sagittarius, activating your 5th house of romance, creativity, and self-expression. This transit brings a playful, adventurous, and optimistic energy to your love life and artistic pursuits. It's a great time to take risks, try new things, and enjoy the pleasures of life.

As the year comes to a close, Jupiter enters Cancer on December 9th, bringing a 12-month cycle of growth, expansion, and opportunities in your 12th house of spirituality, intuition, and inner growth. This transit encourages you to connect with your higher self, explore your subconscious mind, and cultivate a deeper sense of peace and purpose.

Throughout the year, the Saturn-Neptune square will continue to influence your 9th and 12th houses, emphasizing the need for a balance between structure and flow, reality and imagination, in your spiritual and philosophical pursuits. Trust your intuition, stay open to new perspectives, and be willing to let go of limiting beliefs that no longer serve you.

In conclusion, 2025 is a year of personal growth, self-discovery, and new beginnings for Leo. With Mars and the Sun energizing your sign, you'll have the confidence and motivation to pursue your passions and make your dreams a reality. The eclipses and planetary transits will bring changes and opportunities in various areas of your life, from finances and relationships to education and spirituality. Stay true to yourself, embrace your unique qualities, and trust in the journey ahead. The stars are aligned in your favor, Leo, so make the most of this transformative and empowering year!

January 2025

Overview Horoscope for the Month:

January 2025 is a month of fresh starts and new adventures for you, Leo! The year kicks off with Mars, the planet of action and passion, shifting into caring Cancer on the 6th, activating your 12th house of spirituality, solitude and inner growth. You may feel a strong pull to slow down, tune into your intuition, and engage in deep self-reflection. Honor this introspective energy by creating space for meditation, journaling, or creative pursuits that allow you to process emotions and connect with your higher self.

The Full Moon in fellow fire sign Aries on the 13th illuminates your 9th house of travel, higher education and personal growth. You could have a sudden epiphany about a topic you're passionate about learning more or receive an exciting opportunity to broaden your horizons through a trip or new experience. Let your natural curiosity and zest for life be your guide.

Love & Relationships:

With Venus dancing through dreamy Pisces until the 26th, love takes on an ethereal, romantic quality for you this month, Leo. If you're coupled, prioritize quality time with your partner doing activities that inspire you and spark your shared sense of wonder, like attending a poetry reading or trying a new cuisine. You're craving soul-level connection, so don't shy away from intimate conversations about your hopes, dreams and desires.

For single Leos, the stars suggest keeping an open mind and heart. You could meet someone special while exploring a new spiritual practice or creative hobby. Focus more on the feeling of the connection versus surface-level compatibility. Trust what lights you up inside.

When Venus moves into bold Aries on the 27th, the vibe shifts to become more flirty, direct and adventurous. Take the lead in love and don't be afraid to make the first move if you feel a spark. Embrace your confident, charismatic Leo nature!

Career:

Professional matters take a backseat to your personal life and inner world for much of the month, Leo. You'll be more focused on tying up loose ends and completing projects already underway versus pushing ahead on new initiatives. The Capricorn New Moon on the 29th activates your 6th house of work, health and daily routines, providing supportive energy for implementing positive new habits and getting organized. Set realistic goals and break them down into manageable steps.

Your keen intuition can be an asset in business dealings - pay attention to those gut feelings, especially around the Aries Full Moon on the 13th. Behind the scenes research, strategic planning and refining your long-term vision are favored. Be patient and trust that your hard work will pay off in perfect timing.

Finances:

Mercury's retrograde through Capricorn until the 17th could bring some delays or mix-ups in financial matters. Double check statements, be extra clear in money-related communication, and avoid making major purchases or investments if possible. Stick to your budget as best you can.

The second half of January looks more promising for your cash flow. You could receive a bonus, raise or another source of unexpected income around the Aquarius New Moon on the 29th. Focus on the big picture in regards to your finances and be open to innovative money-making ideas. Joining forces with a partner or group could prove profitable.

Health:

Make your physical, mental and emotional well-being a top priority this month, Leo. With Mars in Cancer highlighting your 12th house of rest and healing until mid-April, honor your body's need for downtime and lean into activities that soothe your soul. Gentle movement like yin yoga, time in nature, and creative expression can be especially therapeutic.

You're also more attuned to the mind-body-spirit connection now. Consider exploring holistic healing modalities or spiritually-uplifting practices to support your vitality. Getting a massage, acupuncture treatment or energy work session could provide a much needed recharge.

Travel:

Your appetite for new experiences and adventures comes alive at the Aries Full Moon on the 13th. Plan a weekend trip or book a faraway journey to a destination that's been calling to you. Get off the beaten path and allow space for magic and synchronicity. Solo travel is especially appealing as it offers a chance to fully immerse yourself in a foreign culture and connect with your own rhythms.

If international travel isn't possible, feed your wanderlust through armchair travel - read travelogues set in exotic locales, take a foreign language class, or cook up cuisine from your dream destination. The journey is just as much internal as external this month. Let a shift in perspective be your passport to a wider world.

Insights from the Stars:

January's astrology invites you to balance the dynamic tension between rest and action, Leo. Prioritize solitude and self-care as much as possible, especially while Mars travels through Cancer, but trust your instincts around the Aries Full Moon to take a bold leap of faith. Your curiosity and optimism are your biggest strengths - harness them in service of personal growth and the greater good.

You're learning to honor your sensitivity as a superpower versus a weakness. Embrace your softer side and allow yourself to feel all the feels. Your vulnerability and innate creativity are immensely healing for yourself and others. Let your light shine from the inside out and watch how much more magnetic you become. The world needs your unique Leo magic now more than ever.

Best Days of the Month:

- January 7th: Venus sextile Jupiter. Luck and opportunity are on your side, especially in love and creativity. Indulge in pleasure, pampering and play. Your natural charisma and joie de vivre attract abundance.
- January 13th: Full Moon in Aries. Follow your passions down an exciting new path. You're ready for an adventure of the mind, body or soul. Take a risk, travel or expand your knowledge. Freedom is your keyword.
- January 22nd: Sun enters Aquarius. Focus on partnerships of all kinds and let your quirks and unique personality shine. Brainstorm brilliant ideas with friends and colleagues. Your social life brings exciting surprises.
- January 27th: Venus enters Aries. Turn up the heat on passion projects and pursue what lights you up. Romance takes on a fun, flirty vibe and you're eager to make bold moves. Lead with your heart.

February 2025

Overview Horoscope for the Month:

February 2025 is a dynamic and transformative month for you, Leo! The cosmos are conspiring to help you break free from limitation and chart a bold new course for your future. The month kicks off with a potent Full Moon in your sign on the 12th, putting your desires, creativity and self-expression in the spotlight. Trust your instincts and let your authentic self shine - the world needs your unique light and leadership now more than ever.

Mars, the planet of action and ambition, stations direct in Cancer on the 23rd, ending a two month retrograde that had you focused on internal processing versus external progress. You're feeling re-energized and ready to put insights gained around subconscious patterns and emotional needs into tangible practice. Courage and confidence are your superpowers as the month comes to a close.

Love:

With Venus gracing your 8th house of intimacy and transformation for most of February, relationships take on a deep, soulful quality. You're craving connection that goes beyond the superficial and aren't afraid to have the hard conversations in service of mutual healing and growth. This is an excellent time to address any issues around vulnerability, trust or power dynamics with a partner. For single Leos, an intense attraction could lead to a profound soul connection. Stay open to the magic and synchronicity of the universe playing matchmaker.

Communication planet Mercury moves through your 7th house of partnership from the 14th onward, making it easier to express your needs and listen intently to a loved one. You're able to strike the delicate balance between asserting your individuality and honoring your partner's desires. Shared adventures, stimulating conversation and playful flirtation keep the sparks flying.

Career:

The Aquarius Sun illuminates your 7th house of one-on-one partnerships until the 18th, making this an ideal time for collaborations and joint ventures. Teaming up with a colleague or mentor whose skills complement your own can help you make major strides towards a cherished goal. Your ability to network and connect with influential people is heightened - don't be afraid to reach out and ask for support or opportunities.

The Leo Full Moon on the 12th brings a career matter to fruition or sheds light on your professional path forward. Trust your creativity and unique self-expression to set you apart from the crowd. You're ready to step into the spotlight and take on more responsibility or a leadership role. Just be sure any attention you attract is coming from a place of authenticity versus ego.

Finances:

Money matters get a cosmic boost this month, Leo, thanks to abundant Jupiter moving through your 8th house of shared resources and investments. An inheritance, loan, bonus, tax refund or partner's financial windfall could bless your bank account in unexpected ways. Stay open to receiving and practice gratitude for the abundance flowing your way.

With Venus activating your 8th house until the 27th, it's the perfect time to review or renegotiate joint financial agreements like mortgages, loans or investments. If debt has been an issue, you've got cosmic support to create a repayment plan and stick to it. Combine your creativity and passion with practical planning to manifest prosperity on your own terms.

Health:

Mars retrograde in your 12th house of rest and healing until the 23rd continues to emphasize the mind-body-spirit connection, Leo. Honor your need for extra downtime and make space for activities that soothe and replenish your soul. Journaling, meditation, therapy and creative pursuits can be especially cathartic for processing any heavy emotions that arise.

When Mars stations direct on the 23rd, you may feel a surge of energy and renewed motivation to pursue your wellness goals. Channel this fiery momentum into establishing sustainable self-care routines that support your physical vitality. Get your sweat on with a dance or kickboxing class or take your workouts outdoors to connect with nature's rejuvenating vibes.

Travel:

Your thirst for adventure and new experiences is ignited at the Leo Full Moon on the 12th. Plan a solo getaway or book a bucket-list trip that pushes outside your comfort zone. You're in the mood to take risks, mingle with fascinating people and immerse yourself in foreign cultures. Let your curiosity be your guide.

If long distance travel isn't possible, embrace the power of your imagination as a portal to far-off lands. Read travel memoirs, watch foreign films, take an online class in art history or mythology. Feed your wanderlust from the inside out. A weekend road trip or staycation that takes you off the beaten path could quench your thirst for excitement closer to home.

Insights from the Stars:

February's astro-weather is all about claiming your sovereignty and stepping into your power, Leo. You're being called to shed layers of conditioning and limitation in order to express your most authentic, radiant self. Let go of any masks or personas you've been hiding behind and dare to be unapologetically you. Your vulnerability is your strength.

This is also a powerful month for healing and transformation, particularly around relationships and shared resources. Invite more depth, intimacy and trust into your partnerships by fearlessly communicating your needs and holding space for others to do the same. You're ready to break free from patterns of codependency or self-sabotage in order to manifest soul-nourishing connections.

Best Days of the Month:

- February 12th: Full Moon in Leo. All eyes are on you as you take a bold leap towards a cherished dream. Trust your instincts and creative vision to guide you. Your charisma and star power are undeniable.
- February 16th: Sun sextile Uranus. Expect the unexpected in the best possible way. Exciting opportunities arise that align with your authentic self. Embrace your inner rebel and make a break from the status quo.
- February 19th: Venus sextile Uranus. Surprises and serendipity light up your love life and creativity. An unconventional attraction or innovative idea sets your heart on fire. Embrace the magic of the moment.
- February 23rd: Mars stations direct in Cancer. After two months of introspection, you're ready to charge ahead on passion projects and personal goals. Trust your instincts and channel your emotions into purposeful action. Your persistence pays off.
- February 27th: Venus enters Aries. Romance takes on an adventurous, spontaneous vibe. You're feeling bold and brave in matters of the heart. Take the lead

in love and be direct about your desires. Your confidence is a major turn-on.

March 2025

Overview Horoscope for the Month:

March 2025 is a month of major transitions and new beginnings for you, Leo! The headline news is Saturn, the planet of structure and responsibility, moving into your 9th house of travel, higher education and personal growth on the 24th, where it will stay until February 2028. You're entering a phase of life where you're called to expand your horizons - literally and figuratively - and commit to a path of study or experience that stretches you beyond your comfort zone. Embrace the journey of becoming the most authentic, wise and world-ready version of yourself.

The Aries New Moon on the 29th is also a potent cosmic reset that lands in your 9th house, bringing fresh opportunities for travel, learning and optimistic risk-taking. Set intentions around a bucket-list trip, enrolling in a degree program, or embarking on an entrepreneurial venture. Trust that the universe is conspiring to support your boldest, most courageous moves.

Love:

With Venus in dreamy Pisces activating your 8th house of intimacy and transformation until the 27th, your relationships take on a deeply spiritual, soulful tone this month. You're craving connection that goes beyond the superficial and taps into the realm of unconditional love and acceptance. This is a powerful time for healing any wounds around vulnerability, trust or self-worth that may be blocking you from fully giving and receiving love.

If you're coupled, prioritize quality time with your partner that nourishes your mind, body and soul. A couples' retreat, tantric workshop or shared spiritual practice can deepen your bond. For single Leos, an attraction that feels fated or karmic could sweep you off your feet. Stay open to the magic of divine timing and soul contracts. When Venus moves into Aries on the 27th, your confidence and charisma are amplified. Take the lead in love and be direct about your desires.

Career:

With the Sun illuminating your 8th house of shared resources and investments until the 20th, much of your professional focus is on maximizing joint ventures and collaborations. Teaming up with a business partner, mentor or financial advisor whose skills complement your own can help you make major strides towards a long-term goal. Don't be afraid to ask for support or delegate tasks that fall outside your zone of genius.

The Aries New Moon on the 29th is a powerful time for planting seeds of intention around your career dreams and aspirations. Think big picture and let your entrepreneurial spirit soar. You're ready to take a bold leap of faith towards a path that aligns with your purpose and passions. Trust your instincts and let your unique creative vision be your guide.

Finances:

Money matters continue to be blessed by abundant Jupiter moving through your 8th house of shared resources and investments this month. An unexpected windfall, inheritance, or partner's financial success could boost your bottom line. Stay open to receiving and practice gratitude for the prosperity flowing your way.

With Venus also gracing your 8th house until the 27th, it's an ideal time to review and renegotiate any joint financial agreements, such as loans, mortgages, or investments. If debt has been an issue, you have cosmic support to create a practical repayment plan. Combine your creativity and passion with strategic planning to manifest abundance on your own terms.

Health:

Mars, the planet of energy and action, continues its journey through your 12th house of rest and healing until mid-April, emphasizing the mind-body-spirit connection. Make space for activities that soothe your soul and replenish your energy reserves, such as meditation, yoga, or creative pursuits. If you've been burning the candle at both ends, this is your cosmic cue to slow down and prioritize self-care.

The Aries New Moon on the 29th is a powerful time for setting intentions around your wellness goals and routines. Let go of any self-defeating habits or beliefs that are holding you back and embrace a fresh start. Commit to nourishing your body with wholesome foods, regular movement, and plenty of rest. Remember, your physical vitality is the foundation for everything else in your life.

Travel:

Your wanderlust is ignited this month, Leo, thanks to Saturn's ingress into your 9th house of travel and adventure on the 24th. You're entering a three-year phase where exploring new horizons - both literally and figuratively - is a key theme. Start planning that bucket-list trip or international move you've been dreaming of. Immersing yourself in foreign cultures and perspectives can be incredibly enriching for your personal growth.

If long-distance travel isn't possible just yet, consider signing up for a workshop or retreat that expands your mind and worldview. Even armchair travel, such as reading travelogues or watching documentaries about far-flung places, can satisfy your craving for adventure. The journey is just as much internal as external.

Insights from the Stars:

March's astrology is all about embracing change and stepping into your power, Leo. You're being called to shed limiting beliefs and patterns that are keeping you stuck in your comfort zone. Saturn's move into your 9th house on the 24th is a cosmic push to take responsibility for your personal growth and commit to a path of lifelong learning. Embrace the discomfort of being a beginner and trust that every challenge is an opportunity to expand your wisdom and resilience.

This is also a potent month for healing and transformation, particularly around themes of intimacy, vulnerability, and shared resources. Let go of any fears or defenses that are blocking you from fully giving and receiving love. You're worthy of soul-deep connection and abundant support. Open your heart and trust that the universe has your back.

Best Days of the Month:

- March 11th: Jupiter sextile Uranus. Unexpected opportunities and serendipitous encounters abound. Stay open to the magic of synchronicity and be ready to pivot in a new direction. Your unique skills and quirks are your superpowers.
- March 14th: Full Moon in Virgo. A work project or health matter comes to fruition. Celebrate your progress and release any perfectionist tendencies. Your dedication and attention to detail pay off.
- March 24th: Saturn enters Aries. Commit to a path of study, travel, or personal growth that stretches you beyond your comfort zone. Embrace the journey of becoming the wise, world-ready version of yourself. Patience and persistence are key.
- March 29th: New Moon in Aries. Set intentions for bold new beginnings and adventurous pursuits. Take a leap of faith towards your dreams and trust that the universe will catch you. Your courage and confidence are magnets for success..

April 2025

Overview Horoscope for the Month:

April 2025 is a month of dynamic change and personal growth for you, Leo! The headline news is Pluto, the planet of power and transformation, beginning its 20-year journey through your 7th house of partnership on the 4th. You're entering a long-term cycle where your closest relationships will undergo a profound metamorphosis. This is a time to confront any fears or patterns around intimacy, trust, and shared power that may be holding you back from soul-deep connection. Embrace the journey of learning to love fearlessly and authentically.

The Aries New Moon on the 27th is a powerful cosmic reset that lands in your 9th house of travel, higher education, and personal growth. Set intentions around expanding your horizons through a new course of study, entrepreneurial venture, or bucket-list adventure. Trust your boldest, most visionary ideas and take a leap of faith towards your dreams.

Love:

With the Sun illuminating your 9th house of adventure and higher learning until the 19th, your romantic life takes on an exploratory, philosophical tone. You're attracted to partners who can engage you in stimulating conversation and broaden your perspective. If you're coupled, plan a trip or take a class together that pushes you both outside your comfort zone. The shared experience of learning and growing together can deepen your bond.

Venus, the planet of love and pleasure, graces your 10th house of career and public image from the 30th onwards, bringing a charming, magnetic quality to your professional relationships. Your creative talents and unique self-expression are your superpowers in the workplace. Don't be afraid to showcase your skills and advocate for your worth. A office romance or creative collaboration could also blossom.

Career:

With Mars, the planet of ambition and action, charging through your sign from the 18th onwards, your career goals get a major boost of momentum. You're feeling confident, courageous, and ready to take on new challenges. Trust your instincts and be proactive in pursuing opportunities that align with your passions and purpose. Your leadership skills and entrepreneurial spirit are in the spotlight.

The Taurus New Moon on the 27th is a powerful time for setting intentions around your professional dreams and aspirations. What legacy do you want to leave in the world? Clarify your long-term vision and take practical steps towards making it a reality. Your persistence and determination will pay off.

Finances:

With Pluto beginning its transformative journey through your 7th house of partnership on the 4th, your financial landscape may undergo some shifts in the coming years. This is a time to confront any fears or power struggles around money and shared resources. If you're in a committed relationship, have an honest conversation with your partner about your values and goals. You may need to renegotiate joint financial agreements or create a new budget that works for both of you.

The Aries New Moon on the 27th is a powerful time for setting intentions around abundance and prosperity. Trust that the universe will provide for your needs as you pursue your passions and purpose. Stay open to unexpected sources of income or financial opportunities. Your creativity and innovation are your greatest assets.

Health:

With Mars moving into your sign on the 18th, your physical energy and vitality get a major boost. You're feeling motivated to start a new fitness routine or take on a challenging athletic pursuit. Channel your competitive spirit into reaching your wellness goals, but be mindful not to push yourself too hard too fast. Listen to your body's signals and prioritize rest and recovery.

The Taurus New Moon on the 27th is a powerful time for setting intentions around self-care and nourishment. Commit to healthy habits that support your overall well-being, such as eating whole foods, staying hydrated, and getting plenty of sleep. Indulge your senses with a spa day or nature retreat. When you feel good in your body, everything else in your life flows more smoothly.

Travel:

Your wanderlust is ignited this month, Leo, thanks to the Sun in adventurous Aries activating your 9th house of travel and expansion until the 19th. You're craving new experiences and perspectives that push you outside your comfort zone. Plan a solo trip or book a group tour to a destination that's been on your bucket list. Immersing yourself in foreign cultures and landscapes can be incredibly enriching for your personal growth.

If long-distance travel isn't possible just yet, consider signing up for a workshop or retreat that expands your mind and worldview. Even armchair travel, such as reading travelogues or watching documentaries about far-flung places, can satisfy your craving for adventure. The journey is just as much internal as external.

Insights from the Stars:

April's astrology is all about embracing change and stepping into your power, Leo. Pluto's move into your 7th house of partnership on the 4th is a cosmic push to confront any fears or patterns that may be blocking you from soul-deep intimacy and connection. Trust that the universe is guiding you towards relationships that support your highest growth and evolution. Let go of any masks or defenses and allow yourself to be seen and loved fully.

This is also a potent month for expanding your horizons and taking bold leaps of faith towards your dreams. The Aries New Moon on the 27th is a powerful portal for setting intentions around travel, education, and personal growth. Trust your vision and let your passions be your compass. You have the courage and confidence to navigate any challenges that come your way.

Best Days of the Month:
- April 4th: Saturn sextile Uranus. Unexpected opportunities and innovative solutions arise. Embrace change and think outside the box. Your unique perspective is your superpower.
- April 12th: Full Moon in Libra. A relationship matter comes to a head. Seek balance and compromise. Lead with compassion and strive for win-win solutions.
- April 18th: Mars enters Leo. Your energy, confidence, and charisma are off the charts. Take bold action towards your goals and passions. Your leadership skills are in high demand.
- April 27th: New Moon in Taurus. Set intentions for financial abundance and material security. Clarify your values and commit to practical steps towards your long-term goals. Trust that you have everything you need to thrive.

May 2025

Overview Horoscope for the Month:

May 2025 is a month of exciting opportunities and personal growth for you, Leo! The headline news is Jupiter, the planet of expansion and abundance, forming a supportive sextile aspect to Chiron, the asteroid of healing and wholeness, in your 9th house of travel, higher education, and personal growth on the 18th. This cosmic alignment brings a powerful opportunity to stretch beyond your comfort zone and embrace experiences that support your highest evolution. Trust that the universe is conspiring to help you grow and thrive.

The Gemini New Moon on the 26th is a potent time for setting intentions around communication, learning, and self-expression. You're feeling curious, adaptable, and ready to explore new ideas and perspectives. Embrace your inner student and let your natural charisma shine in social situations. Your unique voice has the power to inspire and uplift others.

Love:

With Venus, the planet of love and pleasure, gracing your 11th house of friendship and community from the 4th onwards, your social life is buzzing with activity. You're feeling popular, magnetic, and ready to connect with like-minded individuals who share your passions and values. Attend events or join groups that align with your interests and let your natural charm and warmth attract new connections.

If you're single, a friendship could blossom into something more romantic around the Gemini New Moon on the 26th. Keep an open mind and heart, and let your playful, flirtatious side shine. If you're coupled, prioritize quality time with your partner doing activities that bring you both joy and laughter. A double date or group outing can refresh your bond.

Career:

With Mars, the planet of ambition and action, charging through your sign all month, your career goals are infused with extra momentum and drive. You're feeling confident, assertive, and ready to take on new challenges in the workplace. Trust your instincts and be proactive in pursuing opportunities that align with your passions and purpose. Your leadership skills and creative vision are your superpowers.

The Gemini New Moon on the 26th is a powerful time for networking and pitching your ideas to others. Your communication skills are in the spotlight, so don't be afraid to speak up and share your unique perspective. A brainstorming session or collaboration with colleagues could lead to a breakthrough.

Finances:

The Scorpio Full Moon on the 12th illuminates your 4th house of home and family, bringing a financial matter to a head. You may need to have an honest conversation with loved ones about your budget, shared resources, or long-term security goals. Trust your intuition and be open to innovative solutions. A home-based business or real estate opportunity could also arise.

With Jupiter and Chiron aligning in your 9th house of expansion and growth on the 18th, you're being called to invest in experiences that stretch you beyond your comfort zone. Consider taking a course or workshop that enhances your skills and increases your earning potential. Trust that the universe will provide for your needs as you pursue your passions and purpose.

Health:

With Mars energizing your sign all month, you're feeling motivated to prioritize your physical health and well-being. Channel your competitive spirit into setting and achieving fitness goals, such as training for a race or trying a new sport. Just be mindful not to push yourself too hard too fast. Listen to your body's signals and incorporate plenty of rest and recovery time into your routine.

The Gemini New Moon on the 26th is a potent time for setting intentions around mental health and self-care. Commit to practices that calm your mind and soothe your nervous system, such as meditation, journaling, or spending time in nature. Engage your curiosity and learn something new that stimulates your intellect. When you feel mentally and emotionally balanced, your physical health flourishes.

Travel:

Your wanderlust reaches a fever pitch this month, Leo, thanks to Jupiter and Chiron aligning in your 9th house of travel and adventure on the 18th. You're craving experiences that expand your horizons and push you outside your comfort zone. Consider booking a trip to a destination that's been on your bucket list or signing up for a study abroad program. Immersing yourself in foreign cultures and perspectives can be incredibly enriching for your personal growth.

If long-distance travel isn't possible right now, seek out opportunities for adventure closer to home. Take a weekend road trip to a nearby town or explore a new neighborhood in your city. Even small shifts in your daily routine can satisfy your craving for novelty and excitement.

Insights from the Stars:

May's astrology is all about embracing growth and stepping into your power, Leo. Jupiter and Chiron's alignment in your 9th house on the 18th is a cosmic invitation to heal any wounds around your sense of purpose and direction. Trust that your unique path is unfolding exactly as it's meant to, even if it looks different than you expected. Let go of any limiting beliefs or fears that are holding you back from pursuing your passions wholeheartedly.

This is also a potent month for expanding your social circle and collaborating with others who share your values and vision. The Gemini New Moon on the 26th is a powerful portal for setting intentions around community, networking, and self-expression. Your voice has the power to inspire and uplift others, so don't be afraid to speak your truth and share your gifts with the world.

Best Days of the Month:

- May 4th: Venus enters Gemini. Your social life is buzzing with activity and connection. Attend events or join groups that align with your passions and let your natural charm shine.

- May 12th: Full Moon in Scorpio. A financial or family matter comes to a head. Trust your intuition and be open to innovative solutions. A home-based business or real estate opportunity could arise.

- May 18th: Jupiter sextile Chiron. Healing and growth opportunities abound, especially around travel, education, and personal development. Invest in experiences that stretch you beyond your comfort zone.

- May 26th: New Moon in Gemini. Set intentions around communication, learning, and self-expression. Your unique voice has the power to inspire and uplift others. Embrace your inner student and let your curiosity lead the way.

June 2025

Overview Horoscope for the Month:

June 2025 is a month of exciting opportunities and personal growth for you, Leo! The headline news is Mars, the planet of action and ambition, moving into your sign on the 17th, where it will stay until late July. This cosmic alignment brings a powerful boost of energy, confidence, and motivation to pursue your goals and desires. You're feeling bold, courageous, and ready to take on new challenges. Trust your instincts and let your natural leadership skills shine.

The Gemini New Moon on the 25th is a potent time for setting intentions around communication, learning, and self-expression. You're feeling curious, adaptable, and eager to explore new ideas and perspectives. Embrace your inner student and let your unique voice be heard. Your words have the power to inspire and uplift others.

Love:

With Venus, the planet of love and pleasure, dancing through your 11th house of friendship and community until the 6th, your social life is buzzing with activity. You're feeling popular, magnetic, and ready to connect with like-minded individuals who share your passions and values. Attend events or join groups that align with your interests and let your natural charm and warmth attract new connections.

When Venus moves into your 12th house of spirituality and inner growth on the 6th, your focus shifts to more introspective pursuits. This is a time to nurture your relationship with yourself and explore the depths of your emotional world. If you're in a committed partnership, prioritize intimate, one-on-one time with your loved one. Heart-to-heart conversations can deepen your bond.

Career:

With Mars charging through your 12th house of behind-the-scenes work until the 17th, much of your professional focus is on tying up loose ends and completing projects that have been on the back burner. Trust your intuition and listen to your inner guidance when making career decisions. Your dreams and subconscious mind hold clues to your true path and purpose.

When Mars moves into your sign on the 17th, your career goals get a major boost of momentum and drive. You're feeling confident, assertive, and ready to take on new challenges in the workplace. Trust your instincts and be proactive in pursuing opportunities that align with your passions and talents. Your leadership skills and creative vision are your superpowers.

Finances:

The Sagittarius Full Moon on the 11th illuminates your 5th house of creativity, self-expression, and play, bringing a financial matter to a head. You may receive recognition or compensation for a creative project or hobby that you're passionate about. Trust your unique talents and let your authentic self shine. Your joy and enthusiasm are your greatest assets.

With Mars moving through your 12th house of hidden resources until the 17th, you may uncover new sources of income or financial support that you weren't previously aware of. Keep an open mind and be receptive to unexpected opportunities. A generous gift or act of kindness from someone in your network could also boost your bottom line.

Health:

With Mars energizing your 12th house of rest and renewal until the 17th, your physical and emotional well-being are in the spotlight. This is a time to prioritize self-care and listen to your body's signals. If you've been burning the candle at both ends, use this opportunity to slow down and recharge your batteries. Engage in activities that bring you a sense of peace and relaxation, such as meditation, yoga, or spending time in nature.

When Mars moves into your sign on the 17th, you'll feel a surge of energy and motivation to pursue your fitness goals. Channel your competitive spirit into trying a new sport or physical activity that challenges you. Just be mindful not to push yourself too hard too fast. Incorporate plenty of rest and recovery time into your routine to avoid burnout.

Travel:

Your wanderlust is activated this month, Leo, thanks to the Sagittarius Full Moon on the 11th illuminating your 5th house of adventure and play. You're craving new experiences and perspectives that expand your horizons and bring you joy. Consider planning a weekend getaway or booking a trip to a destination that's been on your bucket list. Immersing yourself in different cultures and landscapes can be incredibly enriching for your personal growth.

If long-distance travel isn't possible right now, seek out opportunities for exploration and discovery closer to home. Visit a new park or nature reserve, try a foreign cuisine restaurant, or attend a cultural event that broadens your worldview. Even small shifts in your daily routine can satisfy your craving for novelty and excitement.

Insights from the Stars:

June's astrology is all about embracing your authentic self and stepping into your power, Leo. Mars' move into your sign on the 17th is a cosmic invitation to be bold, courageous, and unapologetically you. Trust your instincts and let your unique light shine bright. You have the strength and resilience to overcome any obstacle and achieve your dreams.

This is also a potent month for self-discovery and inner growth. The Gemini New Moon on the 25th is a powerful portal for setting intentions around self-awareness, emotional healing, and spiritual awakening. Take time to reflect on your journey so far and release any limiting beliefs or patterns that are holding you back. You're ready to step into a new chapter of your life with greater wisdom, compassion, and authenticity.

Best Days of the Month:
- June 4th: Venus enters Cancer. Your social life takes on a nurturing, emotional tone. Prioritize quality time with loved ones and

engage in activities that make you feel safe and supported.

- June 11th: Full Moon in Sagittarius. A creative project or passion comes to fruition. Trust your unique talents and let your joy and enthusiasm shine. An adventure or trip could also be on the horizon.
- June 17th: Mars enters Leo. Your energy, confidence, and motivation are off the charts. Take bold action towards your goals and dreams. Your leadership skills and creative vision are your superpowers.
- June 25th: New Moon in Gemini. Set intentions around communication, learning, and self-expression. Embrace your curiosity and let your unique voice be heard. Your words have the power to inspire and uplift others..

July 2025

Overview Horoscope for the Month:

July 2025 is a month of personal growth, self-discovery, and new beginnings for you, Leo! With the Sun, your ruling planet, moving through your sign from the 22nd onwards, you're feeling confident, radiant, and ready to shine your unique light in the world. This is a powerful time to set intentions for the year ahead and take bold action towards your dreams and goals. Trust your instincts and let your natural leadership skills guide the way.

The Leo New Moon on the 24th is a potent cosmic reset that marks the beginning of a new chapter in your personal journey. Set intentions around self-love, creative expression, and authentic living. You're ready to let go of old patterns and beliefs that no longer serve you and step into a more empowered version of yourself. Embrace your inner fire and let your passions be your compass.

Love:

With Venus, the planet of love and pleasure, dancing through your sign from the 25th onwards, your romantic life is infused with extra magnetism and charm. If you're single, this is a wonderful time to put yourself out there and attract new love into your life. Trust your natural charisma and let your authentic self shine. If you're in a committed partnership, prioritize quality time with your loved one doing activities that bring you both joy and laughter. Reignite the spark of passion and playfulness in your connection.

The Leo New Moon on the 24th is a powerful portal for setting intentions around love and relationships. Get clear on the qualities and values you desire in a partner and visualize yourself in a healthy, happy, and fulfilling union. Release any past hurts or resentments that may be blocking you from fully opening your heart. You're worthy of deep, soulful love.

Career:

With Mars, the planet of ambition and drive, charging through your sign all month, your career goals are infused with extra momentum and confidence. You're feeling assertive, proactive, and ready to take on new challenges in the workplace. Trust your creative vision and leadership skills to guide you towards success. This is a fantastic time to launch a new project, pitch your ideas to higher-ups, or take on additional responsibilities that showcase your talents.

The Leo New Moon on the 24th is a potent time for setting intentions around your professional path and purpose. Get clear on your long-term goals and take practical steps towards making them a reality. Believe in yourself and your ability to make a positive impact in the world. Your unique gifts and passions are your greatest assets.

Finances:

The Aquarius Full Moon on the 10th illuminates your 7th house of partnerships and shared resources, bringing a financial matter to a head. If you're in a committed relationship, you may need to have an honest conversation with your partner about your budget, investments, or long-term security goals. Work together to find solutions that feel fair and balanced for both of you. If you're single, this is a good time to review any joint financial agreements or debts and make sure they align with your values and priorities.

With Mars energizing your sign all month, you may feel more motivated to take charge of your finances and pursue new income streams. Trust your entrepreneurial spirit and think outside the box when it comes to generating wealth. Your creativity and innovation are your superpowers.

Health:

With the Sun shining in your sign from the 22nd onwards, you're feeling energized, vital, and ready to prioritize your physical and emotional well-being. This is a wonderful time to start a new fitness routine or health regimen that aligns with your goals and values. Listen to your body's signals and honor its needs for rest, nourishment, and movement. Incorporate activities that bring you joy and make you feel alive, such as dancing, swimming, or hiking in nature.

The Leo New Moon on the 24th is a powerful portal for setting intentions around self-care and personal growth. Commit to practices that support your mental, emotional, and spiritual well-being, such as meditation, journaling, or therapy. Surround yourself with people and environments that uplift and inspire you. When you feel good in your mind, body, and soul, you radiate a magnetic energy that attracts abundance in all areas of your life.

Travel:

Your wanderlust is activated this month, Leo, thanks to the Sun moving through your sign from the 22nd onwards. You're craving new experiences and adventures that expand your horizons and ignite your passion for life. Consider planning a trip to a destination that's been on your bucket list or signing up for a workshop or retreat that supports your personal growth. Immersing yourself in different cultures and perspectives can be incredibly enriching for your mind and soul.

If long-distance travel isn't possible right now, find ways to infuse your daily life with a sense of exploration and discovery. Visit a new neighborhood in your city, try a foreign cuisine restaurant, or attend a cultural event that broadens your worldview. Even small shifts in your routine can satisfy your craving for novelty and excitement.

Insights from the Stars:

July's astrology is all about embracing your authentic self and stepping into your power, Leo. The Sun's move through your sign from the 22nd onwards is a cosmic invitation to celebrate your unique qualities and share your gifts with the world. Let go of any masks or personas that you've been hiding behind and allow yourself to be seen and loved for who you truly are. Your vulnerability is your strength.

The Leo New Moon on the 24th is a powerful portal for setting intentions around self-love, creative expression, and personal growth. Trust that you have everything you need within you to create a life that feels joyful, fulfilling, and abundant. Surround yourself with people and experiences that uplift and inspire you. You're ready to let your inner light shine bright and illuminate the path ahead.

Best Days of the Month:

- July 7th: Uranus enters Gemini. Expect the unexpected in your social life and community. Embrace new friendships and connections that challenge you to think outside the box. Your unique perspective is your superpower.
- July 10th: Full Moon in Aquarius. A partnership or financial matter comes to a head. Work together to find solutions that feel fair and balanced for all involved. Trust your intuition and be open to innovative ideas.
- July 22nd: Sun enters Leo. Happy birthday season, Leo! You're feeling confident, radiant, and ready to shine your unique light in the world. Set intentions for the year ahead and take bold action towards your dreams.
- July 24th: New Moon in Leo. A powerful cosmic reset that marks the beginning of a new chapter in your personal journey. Set intentions around self-love, creative expression, and authentic living. Embrace

your inner fire and let your passions be
your compass.

August 2025

Overview Horoscope for the Month:

August 2025 is a month of personal growth, self-discovery, and new beginnings for you, Leo! With the Sun, your ruling planet, shining in your sign until the 22nd, you're feeling confident, radiant, and ready to take on the world. This is a powerful time to celebrate your unique qualities and share your gifts with others. Trust your instincts and let your natural leadership skills guide the way.

The Aquarius Full Moon on the 9th illuminates your 7th house of partnerships and one-on-one relationships, bringing a significant connection to a turning point. You may need to have an honest conversation with a loved one about your needs, desires, and boundaries. Work together to find solutions that honor both of your individuality and support your growth as a team. If you're single, this could mark the beginning of a new romance or friendship that challenges you to expand your perspective and embrace your authentic self.

Love:

With Venus, the planet of love and pleasure, dancing through your sign from the 13th onwards, your romantic life is infused with extra magnetism and charm. If you're single, this is a wonderful time to put yourself out there and attract new love into your life. Trust your natural charisma and let your authentic self shine. If you're in a committed partnership, prioritize quality time with your loved one doing activities that bring you both joy and excitement. Plan a spontaneous date night or weekend getaway to reignite the spark of passion and adventure in your connection.

Mercury, the planet of communication, will be retrograde in your sign from the 18th onwards, inviting you to reflect on your thoughts, words, and self-expression. This is a good time to review any important conversations or agreements with loved ones and make sure you're on the same page. Be patient with misunderstandings and take time to clarify your intentions. Trust that any challenges are ultimately serving your growth and evolution as a partner and individual.

Career:

With Mars, the planet of ambition and drive, charging through your 2nd house of income and resources until the 22nd, you're feeling motivated to take charge of your finances and pursue new opportunities for growth and abundance. Trust your skills, talents, and value in the workplace. If you've been considering asking for a raise or promotion, this is a favorable time to advocate for yourself and negotiate better terms. You have the power to create the professional life you desire.

When the Sun moves into Virgo on the 22nd, the focus shifts to your 2nd house of money and material resources. This is a good time to review your budget, streamline your expenses, and set clear financial goals for the future. Look for ways to maximize your earning potential and invest in your long-term security. Your hard work and dedication will pay off.

Finances:

The Aquarius Full Moon on the 9th illuminates your 7th house of partnerships and shared resources, bringing a financial matter to a head. If you're in a committed relationship, you may need to have an honest conversation with your partner about your budget, investments, or long-term security goals. Work together to find solutions that feel fair and balanced for both of you. If you're single, this is a good time to review any joint financial agreements or debts and make sure they align with your values and priorities.

With Mars energizing your 2nd house of income and resources until the 22nd, you may feel more motivated to take charge of your finances and pursue new streams of revenue. Trust your entrepreneurial spirit and think outside the box when it comes to generating wealth. Your creativity and innovation are your superpowers.

Health:

With the Sun shining in your sign until the 22nd, you're feeling energized, vital, and ready to prioritize your physical and emotional well-being. This is a wonderful time to continue any fitness routines or health regimens that you started last month. Listen to your body's signals and honor its needs for rest, nourishment, and movement. Incorporate activities that bring you joy and make you feel empowered, such as dancing, swimming, or martial arts.

When Mars moves into Virgo on the 22nd, you may feel a surge of motivation to get organized and streamline your daily routines. This is a good time to declutter your space, both physically and mentally, and make room for new, healthy habits. Focus on small, consistent actions that support your overall well-being, such as eating nourishing foods, staying hydrated, and getting enough sleep. Remember, self-care is not a luxury, but a necessity for your vitality and success.

Travel:

Your wanderlust continues to be activated this month, Leo, thanks to the Sun shining in your sign until the 22nd. You're craving new experiences and adventures that expand your horizons and ignite your passion for life. If you have the opportunity to travel, consider destinations that offer a mix of excitement and relaxation, such as a tropical beach resort or a city with a vibrant cultural scene. Immersing yourself in different environments and perspectives can be incredibly rejuvenating for your mind and soul.

If travel isn't possible right now, find ways to infuse your daily life with a sense of exploration and discovery. Take a day trip to a nearby town or nature reserve, sign up for a class or workshop that teaches you a new skill, or host a foreign movie night with friends. Even small shifts in your routine can satisfy your craving for novelty and excitement.

Insights from the Stars:

August's astrology is all about embracing your authentic self and stepping into your power, Leo. The Sun's journey through your sign until the 22nd is a cosmic invitation to celebrate your unique qualities and share your gifts with the world. Let go of any fears or doubts that may be holding you back from shining your light fully. You are worthy of love, success, and abundance just as you are.

The Aquarius Full Moon on the 9th is a powerful portal for releasing any limiting beliefs or patterns in your relationships that no longer serve your highest good. Trust that by being true to yourself and communicating your needs openly and honestly, you create space for more fulfilling and supportive connections to blossom. Remember, your vulnerability is your strength.

Best Days of the Month:

- August 9th: Full Moon in Aquarius. A significant partnership reaches a turning point. Have an honest conversation about your needs, desires, and boundaries. Work together to find solutions that honor both of your individuality and support your growth as a team.
- August 13th: Venus enters Leo. Your magnetism and charm are off the charts. If single, put yourself out there and attract new love into your life. If coupled, prioritize quality time with your partner doing activities that bring you both joy and excitement.

- August 22nd: Sun enters Virgo / Mars enters Virgo. The focus shifts to your daily routines, health, and work life. Get organized, streamline your schedule, and prioritize self-care. Your hard work and dedication will pay off.
- August 23rd: New Moon in Virgo. Set intentions around your physical and mental well-being, as well as your professional goals. Focus on small, consistent actions that support your overall vitality and success. Trust that you have the power to create the life you desire.

September 2025

Overview Horoscope for the Month:

September 2025 is a month of personal growth, self-reflection, and new beginnings for you, Leo. With the Sun shining in your 2nd house of values, finances, and self-worth until the 22nd, you're being called to reassess your priorities and align your resources with your authentic desires. This is a powerful time to get clear on what truly matters to you and make choices that support your long-term security and happiness.

The Pisces Full Moon on the 7th illuminates your 8th house of intimacy, shared resources, and emotional depth, bringing a significant relationship or financial matter to a turning point. You may need to have an honest conversation with a loved one or business partner about your needs, boundaries, and expectations. Trust your intuition and be open to the transformative power of vulnerability and surrender.

Love:

With Venus, the planet of love and relationships, dancing through your sign until the 19th, your magnetism and charm are off the charts. If you're single, this is a wonderful time to put yourself out there and attract new love into your life. Trust your natural charisma and let your authentic self shine. If you're in a committed partnership, prioritize quality time with your loved one doing activities that bring you both joy and pleasure. Plan a romantic date night or surprise your partner with a thoughtful gesture that shows how much you care.

When Venus moves into Virgo on the 19th, the focus shifts to your 2nd house of values and self-worth. This is a good time to reflect on what you need to feel secure, loved, and appreciated in your relationships. Be honest with yourself and your partner about your emotional and material needs. Work together to create a solid foundation of trust, respect, and mutual support.

Career:

With Mars, the planet of ambition and drive, charging through your 3rd house of communication and ideas from the 22nd onwards, you're feeling motivated to share your thoughts, skills, and expertise with others. This is a fantastic time to network, collaborate, and pitch your ideas to colleagues or clients. Trust your creativity and innovative thinking to help you stand out from the crowd.

The Virgo New Moon on the 21st is a powerful portal for setting intentions around your professional goals and aspirations. Get clear on what you want to achieve in the coming months and take practical steps towards making it a reality. Focus on honing your skills, streamlining your workflow, and delivering high-quality results. Your hard work and dedication will pay off in the form of recognition, rewards, and new opportunities for growth.

Finances:

The Pisces Full Moon on the 7th illuminates your 8th house of shared resources and financial partnerships, bringing a money matter to a head. If you've been considering making a significant investment or negotiating a business deal, this is a good time to trust your intuition and make a decision that aligns with your long-term goals and values. Be open to creative solutions and unexpected sources of support.

With the Sun shining in your 2nd house of income and material security until the 22nd, you're being called to take a closer look at your budget, spending habits, and financial goals. Look for ways to increase your earning potential, save more money, and invest in your future. Remember, your self-worth is not defined by your bank account balance. Focus on cultivating a sense of abundance and gratitude for all the blessings in your life.

Health:

With Mars energizing your 3rd house of communication and mental activity from the 22nd onwards, you may feel a surge of restless energy and a desire to learn, explore, and express yourself. This is a good time to channel your curiosity and enthusiasm into activities that stimulate your mind and keep you physically active, such as hiking, dancing, or trying a new hobby.

The Virgo New Moon on the 21st is a powerful portal for setting intentions around your physical and mental well-being. Focus on creating healthy habits and routines that support your overall vitality and resilience, such as eating nourishing foods, staying hydrated, and getting enough rest. Make time for self-care practices that help you manage stress and maintain a positive outlook, such as meditation, journaling, or spending time in nature.

Travel:

With the Sun shining in your 2nd house of material security and comfort until the 22nd, you may be more inclined to plan a vacation that offers a mix of luxury and relaxation. Consider booking a stay at a high-end resort or spa where you can indulge in pampering treatments, delicious meals, and beautiful surroundings. This is a good time to treat yourself to a little extra TLC and enjoy the fruits of your labors.

When Mars moves into your 3rd house of short trips and local adventures on the 22nd, you may feel a surge of wanderlust and a desire to explore your own backyard. Take a day trip to a nearby town or city, go on a scenic drive, or visit a local attraction that you've always wanted to see. Engaging with your immediate environment can be just as enriching as traveling to far-off destinations.

Insights from the Stars:

September's astrology is all about aligning your resources with your values and cultivating a sense of security and self-worth, Leo. The Sun's journey through your 2nd house until the 22nd is a cosmic invitation to reassess your priorities and make choices that support your long-term happiness and well-being. Let go of any limiting beliefs or habits that are holding you back from feeling abundant, worthy, and fulfilled.

The Pisces Full Moon on the 7th is a powerful portal for releasing any fears, doubts, or emotional baggage that may be blocking your ability to fully trust and surrender in your relationships and financial partnerships. Remember, vulnerability is a strength, not a weakness. By being open and honest about your needs and desires, you create space for deeper intimacy, understanding, and growth.

Best Days of the Month:
- September 7th: Full Moon in Pisces. A significant relationship or financial matter reaches a turning point. Trust your intuition and be open to the transformative power of vulnerability and surrender.
- September 19th: Venus enters Virgo. The focus shifts to your values, self-worth, and material security. Reflect on what you need to feel loved, appreciated, and abundant in your relationships and finances.
- September 21st: New Moon in Virgo. Set intentions around your professional goals, health habits, and personal growth. Focus on creating routines and systems that support your overall vitality, productivity, and success.
- September 22nd: Sun enters Libra / Mars enters Scorpio. The energy shifts towards your relationships, communication skills, and mental activity. Collaborate with

others, express your ideas, and explore new avenues for learning and growth.

October 2025

Overview Horoscope for the Month:

October 2025 is a month of transformation, self-discovery, and new beginnings for you, Leo. With the Sun shining in your 4th house of home, family, and emotional foundations until the 22nd, you're being called to focus on your inner world and create a sense of security and belonging within yourself. This is a powerful time to connect with your roots, honor your feelings, and cultivate a nurturing environment that supports your growth and well-being.

The Aries Full Moon on the 6th illuminates your 9th house of travel, higher education, and personal growth, bringing a significant opportunity or challenge related to your beliefs, adventures, or long-term goals. You may feel a strong urge to break free from your comfort zone and explore new horizons, both literally and figuratively. Trust your instincts and be open to the transformative power of stepping into the unknown.

Love:

With Venus, the planet of love and relationships, dancing through your 3rd house of communication and social connections until the 13th, you're feeling more expressive, curious, and open to meeting new people. This is a great time to network, flirt, and engage in lively conversations with friends, colleagues, and potential love interests. If you're single, you may find yourself attracted to someone who stimulates your mind and makes you laugh. If you're in a committed partnership, prioritize quality time with your loved one doing activities that allow you to learn and grow together, such as taking a class or exploring a new hobby.

When Venus moves into your 4th house of home and family on the 13th, the focus shifts to creating a warm, welcoming, and harmonious environment in your personal life. This is a good time to spend quality time with loved ones, decorate your living space, or host a cozy gathering at home. If there have been any tensions or conflicts in your relationships, this is an opportunity to lead with compassion, understanding, and a willingness to compromise.

Career:

With Mars, the planet of ambition and action, charging through your 4th house of home and family all month, you may feel a strong urge to take charge of your personal life and create a solid foundation for your long-term security and success. This is a great time to assess your work-life balance, set boundaries around your time and energy, and make any necessary changes to your living situation or family dynamics. Trust your instincts and be proactive in creating a supportive environment that allows you to thrive both personally and professionally.

The Libra New Moon on the 21st is a powerful portal for setting intentions around your career goals, public image, and leadership skills. Take some time to reflect on what you want to achieve in the coming months and years, and visualize yourself embodying the qualities of a confident, capable, and inspiring leader. Focus on building strong relationships with colleagues, clients, and mentors who share your values and vision for success.

Finances:

The Aries Full Moon on the 6th illuminates your 9th house of long-term goals and big-picture thinking, bringing a financial opportunity or challenge related to your investments, education, or entrepreneurial ventures. Trust your instincts and be open to taking calculated risks that align with your values and vision for the future. If you've been considering making a major purchase or investment, this is a good time to do your research and seek the advice of trusted experts.

With Venus gracing your 4th house of home and family from the 13th onwards, you may feel inspired to beautify your living space or invest in your long-term security and comfort. This is a good time to review your budget, save money for a rainy day, and make any necessary repairs or upgrades to your home. Remember, your financial well-being is closely tied to your emotional well-being, so focus on creating a sense of abundance, gratitude, and peace in your personal life.

Health:

With the Sun illuminating your 4th house of emotional foundations until the 22nd, you may feel a strong urge to prioritize your mental and emotional well-being this month. This is a great time to focus on self-care practices that help you feel grounded, nurtured, and at peace, such as meditation, therapy, or spending time in nature. If you've been feeling overwhelmed or stressed lately, give yourself permission to slow down, rest, and recharge your batteries.

When the Sun moves into your 5th house of creativity, self-expression, and joy on the 22nd, you may feel a surge of energy and inspiration to pursue activities that light you up from the inside out. This is a great time to engage in hobbies or projects that allow you to express your unique talents and passions, such as art, music, dance, or writing. Remember, play is just as important as work when it comes to maintaining a healthy, balanced lifestyle.

Travel:

The Aries Full Moon on the 6th illuminates your 9th house of travel, adventure, and higher learning, bringing a significant opportunity or challenge related to your desire for exploration and growth. If you've been feeling restless or stuck in a rut lately, this is a great time to plan a trip or embark on a new course of study that expands your horizons and challenges you to step outside your comfort zone. Trust your instincts and be open to the transformative power of immersing yourself in new cultures, ideas, and experiences.

With Mars energizing your 4th house of home and family all month, you may also feel inspired to explore your own backyard and connect with your local community. This is a great time to take a staycation, visit a nearby park or museum, or attend a cultural event that allows you to appreciate the beauty and diversity of your hometown. Remember, sometimes the greatest adventures are the ones that happen closest to home.

Insights from the Stars:

October's astrology is all about creating a strong foundation for your long-term security, happiness, and growth, Leo. The Sun's journey through your 4th house until the 22nd is a cosmic invitation to connect with your roots, honor your emotions, and cultivate a sense of belonging within yourself and your relationships. Trust that by tending to your inner world and personal life, you're laying the groundwork for greater success and fulfillment in all areas of your life.

The Aries Full Moon on the 6th is a powerful portal for releasing any fears, doubts, or limiting beliefs that may be holding you back from pursuing your dreams and reaching your full potential. Remember, growth often involves discomfort and uncertainty, but the rewards are always worth the risk. Trust your instincts, believe in yourself, and take a leap of faith towards the life you truly desire.

Best Days of the Month:

- October 6th: Full Moon in Aries. A significant opportunity or challenge related to travel, education, or personal growth arises. Trust your instincts and be open to stepping outside your comfort zone.

- October 13th: Venus enters Libra. The focus shifts to creating harmony, beauty, and balance in your home and family life. Prioritize quality time with loved ones and make your living space a sanctuary.
- October 21st: New Moon in Libra. Set intentions around your career goals, public image, and leadership skills. Visualize yourself embodying the qualities of a confident, capable, and inspiring leader.
- October 22nd: Sun enters Scorpio. The energy shifts towards creativity, self-expression, and joy. Pursue activities that light you up from the inside out and allow you to express your unique talents and passions.

November 2025

Overview Horoscope for the Month:

November 2025 is a month of creativity, self-expression, and new beginnings for you, Leo. With the Sun shining in your 5th house of romance, joy, and creativity until the 21st, you're being called to embrace your inner child and let your unique light shine brightly. This is a powerful time to pursue your passions, take risks, and express yourself authentically and unapologetically.

The Taurus Full Moon on the 5th illuminates your 10th house of career, reputation, and public image, bringing a significant achievement, challenge, or turning point related to your professional goals and aspirations. You may receive recognition for your hard work and dedication, or feel called to make a bold move in your career that aligns with your true purpose and values. Trust your instincts and be open to the transformative power of stepping into your leadership potential.

Love:

With Venus, the planet of love and relationships, dancing through your 5th house of romance and creativity until the 30th, you're feeling more magnetic, confident, and expressive in your love life. If you're single, this is an excellent time to put yourself out there and attract a partner who appreciates your unique qualities and talents. Be open to playful, spontaneous connections that bring you joy and laughter. If you're in a committed relationship, prioritize fun, passion, and creativity in your interactions with your loved one. Plan a romantic date night, share your hopes and dreams, or work on a creative project together.

Mars, the planet of desire and action, will be charging through your 5th house of romance and self-expression from the 4th onwards, adding even more fire and intensity to your love life. You may feel a strong urge to take the lead in your relationships and go after what you want with confidence and enthusiasm. Just be mindful of coming on too strong or being overly impulsive in your actions. Balance your passion with patience and sensitivity to your partner's needs and feelings.

Career:

The Taurus Full Moon on the 5th illuminates your 10th house of career, reputation, and public image, bringing a significant achievement, challenge, or turning point related to your professional goals and aspirations. You may receive recognition for your hard work and dedication, or feel called to make a bold move in your career that aligns with your true purpose and values. Trust your instincts and be open to the transformative power of stepping into your leadership potential.

With Mars energizing your 5th house of creativity and self-expression from the 4th onwards, you may feel a surge of inspiration and motivation to pursue projects or ideas that showcase your unique talents and skills. This is an excellent time to take risks, think outside the box, and bring your creative vision to life. Just be mindful of overextending yourself or taking on more than you can realistically handle. Focus on quality over quantity and trust that your efforts will pay off in the long run.

Finances:

The Taurus Full Moon on the 5th illuminates your 10th house of career and public image, bringing a financial opportunity or challenge related to your professional goals and aspirations. You may receive a raise, bonus, or new source of income as a result of your hard work and dedication. Alternatively, you may need to reassess your budget or financial priorities to ensure that they align with your long-term goals and values. Trust your instincts and be open to creative solutions and new possibilities for abundance.

With Venus gracing your 5th house of joy and creativity until the 30th, you may feel inspired to invest in experiences or pursuits that bring you pleasure and fulfillment. This is a great time to treat yourself to a hobby or activity that you love, or to splurge on a special item or experience that makes you feel pampered and appreciated. Just be mindful of overspending or indulging in impulsive purchases. Balance your desire for enjoyment with a sense of responsibility and moderation.

Health:

With the Sun illuminating your 5th house of joy and self-expression until the 21st, you may feel a strong urge to prioritize activities and experiences that make you feel alive, energized, and fulfilled. This is a great time to engage in physical activities that you enjoy, such as dancing, sports, or outdoor adventures. You may also feel inspired to express yourself creatively through art, music, or writing as a way to release stress and emotions.

When the Sun moves into your 6th house of health and wellness on the 21st, the focus shifts to creating healthy habits and routines that support your overall well-being. This is a great time to reassess your diet, exercise regimen, and self-care practices to ensure that they are nourishing and sustainable. You may also feel called to be of service to others in some way, such as volunteering for a cause you care about or offering your skills and talents to help someone in need.

Travel:

With Mars energizing your 5th house of adventure and self-expression from the 4th onwards, you may feel a strong urge to travel and explore new horizons this month. This is an excellent time to plan a trip or vacation that allows you to step outside your comfort zone and experience new cultures, ideas, and experiences. You may also feel inspired to take a creative or educational journey, such as attending a workshop or retreat that helps you develop your talents and passions.

If long-distance travel is not possible at this time, consider exploring your local area with a sense of curiosity and wonder. Visit a new neighborhood, try a new restaurant or activity, or attend a cultural event that broadens your perspective and ignites your imagination. Remember, adventure can be found anywhere if you approach life with an open heart and mind.

Insights from the Stars:

November's astrology is all about embracing your inner child, expressing your unique creativity, and taking bold steps towards your dreams and desires, Leo. The Sun's journey through your 5th house until the 21st is a cosmic invitation to let your light shine brightly and unapologetically. Trust that by following your joy and passion, you are aligning with your true purpose and potential.

The Taurus Full Moon on the 5th is a powerful portal for manifesting your professional goals and aspirations, and for stepping into your leadership potential. Remember, success is not just about achieving external recognition or rewards, but about living in alignment with your authentic values and purpose. Trust your instincts, stay grounded in your truth, and be open to the transformative power of embracing your calling.

Best Days of the Month:

- November 5th: Full Moon in Taurus. A significant achievement, challenge, or turning point related to your career and public image arises. Trust your instincts and be open to stepping into your leadership potential.
- November 4th: Mars enters Sagittarius. The energy shifts towards adventure, exploration, and personal growth. Take risks, expand your horizons, and pursue experiences that ignite your passion and curiosity.
- November 21st: Sun enters Sagittarius. The focus shifts to health, wellness, and service. Create healthy habits and routines that support your overall well-being, and find ways to be of service to others.
- November 30th: Venus enters Capricorn. Your love life takes on a more serious, committed tone. Focus on building strong, stable relationships based on mutual respect, trust, and shared values..

December 2025

Overview Horoscope for the Month:

December 2025 is a month of introspection, transformation, and new beginnings for you, Leo. With the Sun shining in your 6th house of health, wellness, and service until the 21st, you're being called to focus on your daily routines, habits, and practices that support your overall well-being. This is a powerful time to reassess your priorities, let go of what no longer serves you, and create a strong foundation for your personal and professional growth.

The Gemini Full Moon on the 4th illuminates your 11th house of friendships, community, and future vision, bringing a significant realization, opportunity, or turning point related to your social connections and long-term goals. You may feel a strong urge to connect with like-minded individuals who share your values and aspirations, or to take a bold step towards manifesting your dreams and ideals. Trust your intuition and be open to the transformative power of collaboration and innovation.

Love:

With Venus, the planet of love and relationships, dancing through your 6th house of service and daily routines until the 24th, you may find yourself drawn to partnerships that are grounded in practicality, stability, and mutual support. This is a great time to focus on the daily habits and rituals that nurture your closest relationships, such as cooking meals together, running errands, or tackling household projects. If you're single, you may feel attracted to someone who shares your values and work ethic, or who inspires you to be your best self.

When Venus moves into your 7th house of partnerships on the 24th, the focus shifts to creating harmony, balance, and beauty in your one-on-one relationships. This is a wonderful time to deepen your connection with your significant other through heartfelt conversations, shared adventures, and acts of love and appreciation. If you're single, you may feel ready to attract a soulmate connection or take a existing relationship to the next level. Trust your heart and be open to the magic of love and romance.

Career:

With Mars, the planet of ambition and drive, energizing your 6th house of work and service all month, you may feel a strong urge to take charge of your professional life and make meaningful contributions to your community or industry. This is an excellent time to tackle projects that require focus, discipline, and attention to detail, or to take on a leadership role that allows you to mentor or guide others. Just be mindful of overextending yourself or taking on more than you can realistically handle. Balance your desire to be of service with a commitment to self-care and boundary-setting.

The Capricorn New Moon on the 19th is a powerful portal for setting intentions related to your career, reputation, and public image. Take some time to reflect on your long-term goals and aspirations, and visualize yourself achieving success and fulfillment in your chosen path. Focus on building strong relationships with colleagues, clients, and mentors who support your growth and development, and trust that your hard work and dedication will pay off in the long run.

Finances:

The Gemini Full Moon on the 4th illuminates your 11th house of hopes, dreams, and community, bringing a financial opportunity or challenge related to your long-term goals and aspirations. You may receive unexpected support or resources from a friend, group, or organization that shares your values and vision. Alternatively, you may need to reassess your budget or financial priorities to ensure that they align with your true purpose and passions. Trust your intuition and be open to creative solutions and new possibilities for abundance.

With Venus gracing your 6th house of work and service until the 24th, you may find opportunities to increase your income or receive recognition for your skills and talents in the workplace. This is a great time to focus on developing your expertise, networking with colleagues, and taking on projects that showcase your value and contributions. Just be mindful of overworking yourself or neglecting your personal life in the pursuit of financial gain. Balance your desire for success with a commitment to self-care and enjoyment.

Health:

With the Sun illuminating your 6th house of health and wellness until the 21st, you're being called to prioritize your physical, mental, and emotional well-being this month. This is an excellent time to reassess your self-care practices, diet, exercise routine, and stress management techniques to ensure that they are nourishing and sustainable. You may feel inspired to try a new healing modality, such as acupuncture or massage, or to incorporate more mindfulness and relaxation into your daily life.

When the Sun moves into your 7th house of partnerships on the 21st, the focus shifts to creating balance and harmony in your relationships. This is a great time to prioritize quality time with loved ones, engage in activities that bring you closer together, and practice the art of compromise and communication. Remember, taking care of yourself is not selfish, but rather a necessary foundation for being able to show up fully and authentically in your relationships.

Travel:

With Mars energizing your 6th house of work and service all month, you may find yourself traveling for business or professional development purposes. This is an excellent time to attend conferences, workshops, or training programs that help you expand your skills and knowledge in your field. You may also feel called to take a service-oriented trip, such as volunteering for a cause you care about or participating in a community project.

If personal travel is on your agenda, consider destinations that offer a blend of relaxation, adventure, and cultural enrichment. You may be drawn to places that have a strong connection to nature, spirituality, or history, or that allow you to immerse yourself in new experiences and perspectives. Trust your intuition and be open to the transformative power of stepping outside your comfort zone and embracing the unknown.

Insights from the Stars:

December's astrology is all about creating a strong foundation for your personal and professional growth, Leo. The Sun's journey through your 6th house until the 21st is a cosmic invitation to get grounded in your daily routines, habits, and practices that support your overall well-being. Trust that by taking care of the details and practicalities of life, you are setting yourself up for long-term success and fulfillment.

The Gemini Full Moon on the 4th is a powerful portal for manifesting your hopes, dreams, and ideals, and for connecting with like-minded individuals who share your vision and values. Remember, you are not alone on your journey, and there is strength and magic in collaboration and community. Trust your intuition, speak your truth, and be open to the transformative power of innovation and imagination.

Best Days of the Month:
- December 4th: Full Moon in Gemini. A significant realization, opportunity, or turning point related to your friendships, community, and future vision arises. Trust your intuition and be open to the power of collaboration and innovation.
- December 19th: New Moon in Capricorn. Set intentions related to your career, reputation, and public image. Focus on building strong relationships and trust that your hard work and dedication will pay off.
- December 21st: Sun enters Capricorn. The focus shifts to partnerships, balance, and harmony. Prioritize quality time with loved ones and practice the art of compromise and communication.
- December 24th: Venus enters Aquarius. Your love life takes on a more unconventional, adventurous tone. Be open to new experiences and perspectives in

your relationships, and trust the magic of
serendipity and synchronicity.

Made in United States
Orlando, FL
12 December 2024

55468573R10065